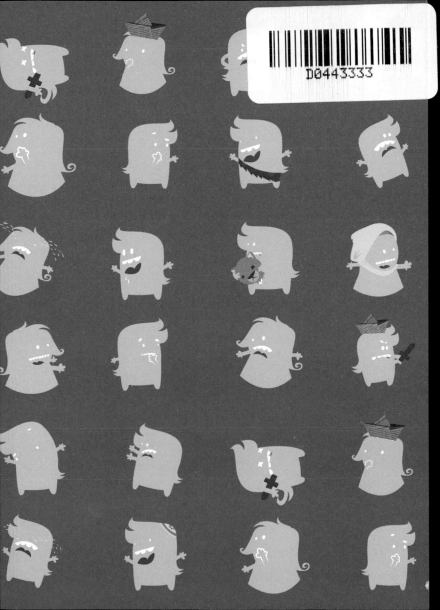

Originally published in Dutch by Uitgeverij Snor
© 2011 Uitgeverij Snor
All rights reserved
Published in English by Who's There LLC
Venice, CA 90291
knockknockstuff.com

Edited translation © 2015 Who's There LLC
All rights reserved
Knock Knock is a trademark of Who's There LLC
Made in China

The rights to this book have been negotiated by the
literary agency Sea of Stories, www.seaofstories.com

Original text: Suzanne Rethans
Concept and assistance: Claudette Halkes and Annemarieke Piers
Design and artwork: Job, Joris & Marieke

ISBN: 978-160106667-1
UPC: 82570350043-1

10 9 8 7 6 5 4 3 2 1

Little Philosophers, Big Questions!

Answers to life's mysteries
for kids & their grownups

KNOCK
KNOCK®
VENICE, CALIFORNIA

Table of Contents

A Note to Grownups

Children will ask just about anything. That's great, but it can also be tough when you don't have answers to their many profound philosophical questions—and still don't after hours of Googling.

All that's in the past, though. Now you can just say, "Let's look it up." Because all the answers to the really tricky questions are here in this little book. Presented by experts. With cute illustrations.

But this book isn't just for kids. Everybody has questions about this stuff, and with this book, parents and kids can ponder the big questions together, and decide which answers are right for them. There's no single answer to these questions; you can look at them from many angles. Do you want a religious approach, or do you prefer a scientific or philosophical explanation? This book will help you teach your child to make his or her own choices.

I had a great time working on this book, and it paid off immediately. When my son started asking questions like "Is there anyone else just like me?" I was able to introduce him to the concept of individuality. Suddenly, I knew how to briefly explain how the world had come into existence. And when he started to get smug about his knowledge of dinosaurs and laughed at me because I couldn't immediately name the carnivores ("Just look at the teeth, Mom!"), I was able to turn around and ask him, "Yes, but can animals fall in love?"

Ha!

That's why I dedicate this book to my children, Mees and Tijl.

—*Suzanne Rethans*

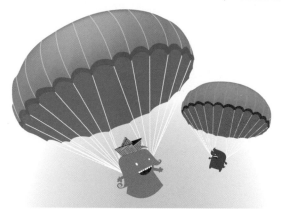

The Experts

This book offers perspectives from a diverse range of individuals who generously shared their time, wisdom, and expertise.

♀ The Biologist

Midas Dekkers is a Dutch biologist and author of fiction and nonfiction books for children and adults.

? The Philosopher

René Gude was editor in chief of the Dutch magazine *Filosofie*, and is now director of the International School of Philosophy in Leusden, the Netherlands.

René Gude: "Children are not too stupid for anything, and they're certainly not too stupid to think about the important issues in this book. But it's also good for me to contemplate these things along with them. Older people often pretend they already know something and act like they're over and done with pondering difficult issues. While philosophy can be a lot of fun and very profitable, it takes courage to admit that you don't know something. Children are very good at this, and that helps me."

 The Brain Expert

Mark Mieras is a physicist and science journalist specializing in the study of the brain. He has authored a book on brain research and a book answering 200 physical science questions.

Mark Mieras: "Brain research tells us a lot about ourselves. I think it's very important that this information does not remain hidden in scientific magazines. Brain research often gives very concise answers to very real questions, from adults as well as children."

🪐 *The Astronomer*

Govert Schilling is a science journalist and editor in chief of the website All about Astronomy (Alles Over Sterrenkunde). He writes articles about astronomy and space research, and has written more than thirty books.

Govert Schilling: "What could be more fun than answering inquisitive questions from children? It's fantastic that, as a parent, you can get help from this book."

✂ *The Pastor*

Harrie Brouwers has studied philosophy and theology. When he has a lot of kids at his services, he likes to give a summary of the proceedings for kids in language they understand. He even does this when there aren't many kids present. The grownups ask for it.

Harrie Brouwers: "Parents and kids are letting a chance go by if they avoid interesting questions of a philosophical nature. It's a joy to philosophize with children. And perhaps this book can help to do that!"

✡ *The Rebbetzin (Rabbi's Wife)*

Bracha Heintz is married to Rabbi Aryeh Leib Heintz. Bracha has studied Hebrew and Jewish philosophy, and has taught children and adults in England, the United States, and the Netherlands. Several times a week, adults and children come to her house to be introduced to Judaism. Bracha knows a lot about kids: she has eleven children and three grandchildren!

Bracha Heintz: "I love to give information about G-d and His creative power to everybody who is interested."

✸ *The Buddhist*

Willem Scheepers is a Zen Buddhist and works as a teacher and coordinator with the Zentrum, a Zen educational and counseling center in the Netherlands. He is married and has two daughters.

Willem Scheepers:
"As adults, perhaps we don't
ask ourselves many questions
anymore; so many things

appear to be obvious or matter-of-fact. But the questions do exist, and children show us that all that questioning starts at a young age—and is in fact part of us. Answering questions from children forces you to give the clearest possible answer, without trimmings, mystifications, and pomposity. That's not easy, but it's enlightening."

♥ *The Cardiologist*

Pim van Lommel was a cardiologist for over twenty-five years at a large teaching hospital, and in 1986 began studying near-death experiences in patients who had suffered a cardiac arrest. He is the author of the book *Consciousness Beyond Life: The Science of the Near-Death Experience.*

● *The Dream Expert*

Lia Timmer studied psychology and is a dream expert. She gives lectures and workshops about dreams, and she helps children interpret their dreams.

Lia Timmer: "I have experienced in my own life what an enormous positive addition dreams can be. They offer support in overcoming fears, which results in more self-confidence! It's better to start as early as possible to take our dreams seriously."

◼ The Sleep Expert

Victor Spoormaker is a sleep researcher and author of two popular scientific books about sleeping. He works at the Max Planck Institute for Psychiatry in Munich.

Victor Spoormaker: "The great thing about this book, in my opinion, is the fact that its guiding principle is curiosity. It's not about preconceived notions or strong convictions, but just about having an open mind—and open questions. That's the best way to understand the world around you."

◕ The Cabaret Performer

Youp van 't Hek is a cabaret performer and newspaper columnist. He's also the father to three children, and has loved telling them stories since they were very small. He is the author of a children's book based on these stories.

◂ The Psychologist

Nico Frijda is professor emeritus at the University of Amsterdam. He has spent his entire career studying human emotions. He wrote *The Laws of Emotions*, among other books.

Nico Frijda: "I always love talking about emotions and explaining them, and I'm sure that the subject can be explained to children in ways they will find interesting. The explanations in this book may be of help to them."

☪ *The Imam*

Abdulwahid van Bommel teaches at the Islamic University Rotterdam, and gives lectures and writes books about Islam.

Imam Abdulwahid van Bommel: "When you talk a lot with adults about faith, it's a challenge to make things comprehensible for children. Actually, we should always talk and write in a way that's understandable for children. That's true communication."

Chapter 1
The Beginning

Let's begin our discussion at the beginning of the beginning of the start of everything, or even just a little bit before that.

The Astronomer:

The Earth is a planet that revolves around the sun, along with the other planets in our solar system. We now know, more or less, how the solar system was created. But we don't know how the universe was created. The only thing we have learned is what things probably looked like a very long time ago, when everything had just started.

Imagine if an alien from another planet came down to Earth to see how humans came into existence. He might see a wrinkled newborn baby, but he still wouldn't have any idea how the baby came out of its mother's belly, let alone how it got in there in the first place. It's the same thing when we're trying to figure out how the universe began, and what might have happened before that caused it to come into existence.

The Big Bang

The universe is continuously expanding, as we discovered in the last century. And because we know this, we can reason backward. If the universe is continuously expanding, that means that in the past, it was all much closer together. If everything was close together, it must have been very hot. So it would appear that the universe came into being with some kind of giant, hot explosion. And that giant, hot explosion is what we call the Big Bang. We think the Big Bang happened almost 14 billion years ago.

Atoms

This Big Bang caused very small particles called atoms to come into existence, and they spread themselves across the universe. But these particles weren't spread out evenly: gravity made them clump together. These clumps became bigger and bigger, just like snowballs, and they eventually became galaxies. Galaxies are large, pancake-shaped collections of stars and planets. In galaxies, matter also clumps together, and that's how stars are created. Often there are more than 100 billion stars in a single galaxy.

Rotating disk

Our galaxy is called the Milky Way. And our sun is one of its stars. At first, there was a rotating disk of gas and dust around the sun. Inside that disk, everything started clumping together due to the force of gravity. This is how the planets in our solar system, including the Earth, came into existence. The Earth is around 4.6 billion years old, almost as old as the sun. Other stars also have planets; our sun and Earth are not unique in that. And with new stars, those rotating disks of gas and dust have also been seen. So in the future, this may also lead to the creation of new planets around those stars.

? *The Philosopher:*

We don't know exactly how the Earth was created because we weren't there. "Knowing" is connected to "experiencing." Through experience, you know what is happening. Well, we weren't around to experience the creation of the Earth. We can only guess how it happened. We use large telescopes to look into space and see the light from stars that you can't see with the naked eye. With large dish-shaped antennas, we can collect radio waves of things that happened far away. Strangely enough, this can help us learn a lot about the past. Those light beams and radio waves take a long time to arrive. Sometimes it takes millions of years before they reach us. It is possible that we might look at light from a star that actually was extinguished long ago. So we can actually see things that happened a long time ago.

This is how scientists agreed on the idea of the Big Bang, an enormous explosion when the universe came into existence. In the past, other ideas existed in science and philosophy, but nowadays philosophers wait quietly until scientists with their large telescopes give us more news. And as soon as scientists prove that in fact the Big Bang really did happen, there will probably be a curious philosopher who will ask, "What exploded in the Big Bang, and where did it come from?"

✡ *The Rebbetzin:*

In school, there is the idea that we understand everything and can explain everything. And if there is something that we can't explain, then we have theories. But that isn't the same thing as proof! That is just drawing a line between A and B, and continuing in the same way to C.

When G-d created everything, He did not put man on Earth as a baby, but as an adult person. And if you had cut down a tree on the day of creation, then you would have been able to count the age rings. G-d created the world in a mature state, with mountains and rivers. He did that in six days, but who says that those days had the same length as our days? Perhaps every day lasted as long as 10 million years. Or perhaps

G-d made things in one day that would normally take 10 million years to come into existence.

☪ *The Imam:*

In the Koran, the creation of everything that exists, and what we can see and understand about it all, is interconnected. Creation took place in six time periods, but these time periods were not necessarily days as we know them. It is said that for God, one day might last 5,000 years. The entire world and the heavens are there for us to look at and think about; the transition from day to night, the tides, the seasons. God created man, his representative on the Earth, from clay or loam. He shaped him in the correct proportions. But man is different, because Allah did not only shape him, but also breathed something from His own spirit (or "ruh") into him.

How did life on Earth start?

🪐 *The Astronomer:*

People are made up of atoms, and those atoms were created in the center of stars. That means that we're actually made of stardust!

During the Big Bang, the two simplest atoms were created: hydrogen and helium. After stars began to form, other atoms were created in their centers: oxygen, carbon, and iron.

When a star explodes, these materials appear in space. Our solar system was created from an exploding star, and that's why it contains oxygen, carbon, and iron, the substances that also appear in our bodies. All of life is a coincidental composition of atoms, including the atoms in your body. When you die, these atoms do not cease to exist.

Atoms have almost eternal life. When your body decomposes in the Earth, or when you are cremated, they are released into the air. That's how you will always float around somewhere.

C★ *The Imam:*

Because there are all types of mysterious things in the Koran that you can't immediately understand, Muslims don't really know for sure how life on Earth came into existence. The Koran asks, "Have not those who disbelieve known that the heavens and the earth were joined together as one united piece, then We parted them? And We have made from water every living thing . . . And We have made the heaven a roof, safe and well guarded . . . And He it is Who has created the night and the day, and the sun and the moon, each in an orbit floating." Scholars also think that all life most likely came from water. The Koran calls the original existence only a mass of gas—"dukhan"—which at first was compact, and then was separated. It has also been said that heaven and Earth were created "and all that is between them." This could mean the layers of matter outside the organized astronomical systems. Of course, it could also simply mean: all that is between heaven and Earth.

The Astronomer:

That's very possible. The building blocks of life, atoms, are everywhere in the universe. So it's absurd to think that there would only be life on Earth. But it's just not very probable that there would be people on other planets. Human evolution, and what we look like now, is in fact pure coincidence. Many biologists believe that if everything were to happen again, there wouldn't necessarily be dinosaurs, or people. Maybe completely different life forms would emerge. It's very possible that the evolution on other planets would lead to the creation of very different life forms. So far, we've found over 200 planets near other stars. A planet near the star Gliese 581 somewhat resembles Earth. Not too hot and not too cold. Perhaps there could be life on that planet.

Are *we* descendants of the apes?

∝ *The Pastor:*

You should always answer "yes" when you're asked this question. First of all, because it's true, and second of all, because it's fun. I always tell children about my visit to the Apenheul Primate Park. When you walk around there for a while, you no longer see the difference between small children and monkeys. At most, there's a very small difference. But otherwise, they behave the same. At one point, I saw a little boy squatting next to a little monkey, and he offered him a handful of grass. The monkey had a look at the pieces of grass, then grabbed the boy's glasses and ran off. That's the difference between men and apes—the capacity for friendship and love. You can only become a human being when you're able to put yourself in someone else's position. When you can imagine what the other needs, or cry for his or her sadness.

The Biologist:

No, we are not descendants of the apes; we *are* apes. If there were life on Mars and a special envoy were to land on Earth to take animals for a zoo on Mars, the humans would be put together with the apes, without a doubt. They would think: that one monkley is a bit bald, but other than he's just like the others. And wow, he even likes bananas!

The Astronomer:

The idea of evolution is hard to grasp for someone who's visiting the zoo, who might be wondering, "Am I a descendant of that orangutan over there scratching his butt?" No, it's not like that. We aren't the descendants of chimpanzees or orangutans; we're the descendants— just like them—of the same ancestor. That ancestor was probably a primitive kind of ape. So actually we're distant cousins. You may be very different from your own cousins, so you can imagine that 7 million years would result in enormous differences. That's how long ago our common ancestor lived.

In some ways, 7 million years is a very long time, but in some ways, it's not so very long. Think of it this way. Imagine standing on the sidewalk with your mom, holding hands. Let's say each yard of the sidewalk represents one generation. After walking 250-300 miles or so, you'd be back at the common ancestor of apes and humans. That's about the distance from Los Angeles to Las Vegas. If you traveled that distance by car, a trip of a few hours, you would see all the descendants up to that common ancestor.

☾ *The Imam:*

Some thoughts will always fascinate people—for example, the famous caption under a painting of a pipe by René Magritte that reads, "This is not a pipe." Imagine a picture of a human being with the caption, "This is not an ape." How do we know whether we are apes? Science tells us we came from apes, but there are no living witnesses, and no apes becoming human beings in the zoo. Does reality exist when we can't see it? For a Muslim, the question is: are you prepared to adjust your faith to science? Muslims try, from a certain sense of wonder and intuition, to match such a developmental story with the Creation narrative.

We can see that humans demonstrate monkeylike behavior. And Islam does consider man a talking animal.

When did humans first appear?

The Biologist:

It depends what you consider the beginning of humans. One theory is that people used to have hair all over and live in trees. At some point, we lost all that hair and came down from the trees, because the climate changed. Forests changed into savannas—grasslands with a tree here and there. It was hot, and we had to find a way to cool ourselves down—by sweating. But sweating only works when you don't have a lot of hair. Those savannas are still in our genes. Man isn't actually made for busy cities: he wants grasslands, with a tree here and there! That's why we make parks.

Another theory is that when we were still apes, we began to live near water. When you live on the beach, you want to get in the water, and when you're in the water very often, then you'll lose your hair. Look at whales and seals. Hair doesn't help you under the water, but fat does. And that's what you see with people. A lot of fat, not a lot of hair. So it all depends which period you pick in the development of humankind.

🪐 *The Astronomer:*

All life began with little atoms which at some point formed molecules, and then evolved to single-celled organisms. And these in turn also evolved. A lot of things have evolved, but a lot have also become extinct. Evolution is a very slow process. From 4 billion years of life on Earth, for at least 2 billion years there were only single-celled organisms—bacteria and such. In the last 500 million years enormous developments have occurred, from the plant kingdom to fish and amphibians. Something like the human species hasn't been around that long. Most species and organisms come and go, and stay for several million years. Crocodiles have been around for over 200 million years, but you probably won't see human beings around in 50 million years.

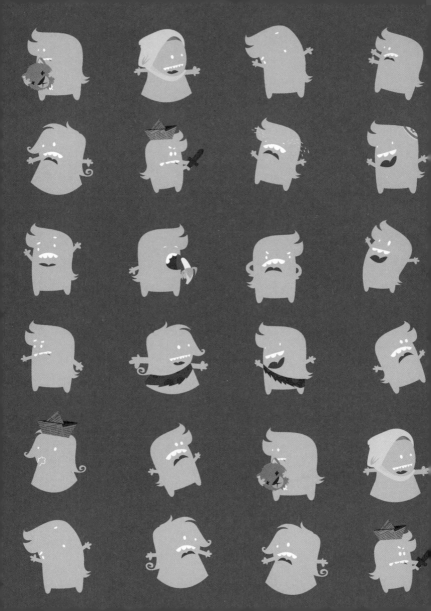

A Word of Thanks

Thanks to all the experts who participated so generously in the creation of this book. Most of all thanks to you, the children and grownups who read it, and who work together to figure out the big questions we all share.

Notes

Notes

Chapter 2
Animals

Animals are a bit like people.
That's probably because people
are animals, too.

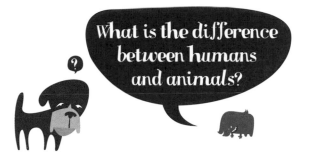

The Biologist:

The difference between humans and animals is no greater than the difference between one animal and another animal. Each species is unique. We humans think that we're very different because we have more brains. But if we were giraffes, we would think we were different from all other animals because of our long necks. Millipedes think they're the best because they have the most legs. But the fact remains that there is a vast gap between humans and animals. And when you ask what this gap is, you'll hear theories that all prove to be nonsense. For example, for a long time we thought we were the only species that used tools. But then we found out that chimpanzees in the woods use sticks to fish for termites.

The most significant difference between humans and animals can be seen in the zoo. Humans walk on one side of the bars, and all the other animals are on the other side. We have to pay to see them; they can look at us for free. But those bars aren't there for nothing. If you were to remove them, you would not see any visitors the next day. At the moment, humans are the most powerful, and we demonstrate that by putting lions and tigers in cages. In the meantime, we run the risk of dying from tiny bacteria. We don't have cages small enough, so we are still being threatened by nature.

? *The Philosopher:*

Animals are better at some things than humans, such as smelling (dogs), or seeing (eagles). Animals can use tools—for example, using a stick to get fruit from a tree.

But people can make tools to make tools. Without a needle and thread, you can't make warm clothes with sleeves, hoods, and buttonholes. There would be no Eskimos, or even North Americans, if no one had thought of coming up with such a small pointy thing with a hole in it. Fantastic. But it's also tricky, because now we're so good at making cars, boats, and planes with our tools that it completely changes nature.

Perhaps it will soon be so warm you'll be able to sunbathe in Greenland and there won't be a North Pole. And what's the Arctic without igloos?

The biggest difference between us and animals is what we can do with language. Animals such as bees and dolphins also have languages, but with humans, language has really gotten out of hand. We talk all day long, with or without cell phones, and we can also write down what we're saying. We can talk about things that don't exist yet (imagination), things that will never exist (fantasy), and things that happened in the past (memory). And it's difficult at the same time, because we can also lie or misunderstand each other.

✡ *The Rebbetzin:*

Humans can talk, and animals can't. A man can keep his thoughts above his feelings; an animal can't. When an animal feels like doing something, it'll just go and do it. An animal does not have the power to reject his instincts.

☾ *The Imam:*

There are clear differences in development between humans and animals—in the ways we think, act, and use language. We humans can fantasize, imagine something, and empathize with others. Animals

aren't able to do that. In religious doctrine a human is a thinking and talking animal, an animal with some kind of logic. We are mammals—but with a diploma. In this context, Muslims think about the source of good and evil. How can humans and other animals distinguish this? Islam assumes that humankind is essentially good. Man has a conscience because of a divine spark. Chimpanzees, on the other hand, correct their bad behavior because they react to their surroundings. In humans this happens more through rules, values, and ideals. That's how you can achieve an understanding of good and evil.

Can animals talk?

The Biologist:

The big difference between humans and animals, and what makes us so powerful, is our language. Thanks to our language we can build rockets, bridges, and cages in zoos. Animals are also very good at communicat-

ing with each other, but they do it in a different manner. And because we're not really looking, we don't notice it. An animal is very good at smelling, and the smell of dog poop can tell another dog exactly who left it there, whether it's from a male or a female dog, and if that dog wants to mate. For a dog, a single piece of poop is a message, three poops are a memo, and a park filled with poop is an entire library. When a dog has been for a walk, he is up to date with all the neighborhood gossip. We've lost our sense of smell, so we think that animals don't communicate. But they talk all the time.

A dog can leave a piece of poop behind and after three days it will still be there, with the entire story it contains. You may wonder why animals don't have a language like we do. Simply put, they don't need it. All animals can do what they need in life. If they can't do something, they don't need it.

☪ *The Imam:*

You could also ask yourself whether we humans know how to talk. We try to, but do we really understand each other? We have several types of language in common with animals, such as body language, eye contact, body odor, mouth odor. All this can express whether we want to interact. There's a question about language which is very similar to the

question about the soul: is language an inherent skill or is it taught? That mystery is why we love the story of Tarzan so much—a man who grows up without human language. For Jane, "Me Tarzan, you Jane" was enough to make her fall in love.

Can you talk with animals?

The Biologist:

When a person talks to an animal, he usually does it in his own language. But when you speak English, it doesn't mean that an animal will understand you. I actually know that cats only speak French, and dogs speak German. If you want to try to learn the language of animals, you should listen carefully to what an animal says. And I don't mean sounds, but smells and body language. If you really want to get to know a dog, you should put your nose under his tail. Animals demonstrate in many different ways what their moods are. When you understand this language, then you have real contact.

We are apes, but the big difference between us and the other apes is that we talk and they don't. What do apes do? They groom each other. When you listen carefully to people's speech, you'll notice that ninety-nine percent is nonsense meant only to strengthen the social bond. "Hi, good morning, how are you?" Apes do exactly the same when they're grooming. They'll groom one ape but not another, and this demonstrates their friendly ties. Hairdressers groom and talk at the same time, so that's actually double.

☪ *The Imam:*

The Muslim world has many stories with talking animals. The Koran says that people can talk with animals. For example, Solomon, David's son, says in the Koran, "Oh people, we were taught the language of birds." He understood and spoke the language of birds, but also the language of much smaller animals such as ants. When he marched with his army through the valley, he heard an ant say, "Oh ants, crawl into your nests, otherwise Solomon and his armies will crush you and they will not even notice it." When he heard this, Solomon smiled at her words and was surprised that he understood them. One day, he asked an ant how much she ate in a year. She said that one corn kernel was enough. Solomon decided to see if the ant was speaking the truth, and he put her in a bottle with a corn kernel.

After a year, he looked inside the bottle and saw that the ant had eaten half of the kernel. "You told me that you eat an entire kernel of corn in a year," Solomon said. "That's when I rely on God," said the ant, "but now that I get my food from you, I keep half as reserve."

Which animal is most like a human?

The Biologist:

It all depends on the way you look at it. Many people will say a monkey. And that's true, we're related. But when you look at way of life, we also resemble pigs, who are opportunistic omnivores.

The Philosopher:

Monkeys are most similar to humans, especially the bonobo.

Can animals laugh, think, and fall in love?

The Biologist:

There's no fundamental difference between humans and animals; they can do everything that we can do. Butterflies lure each other with a special substance. Females release a substance that males can smell miles away. The male doesn't think, "That's a luring substance." He thinks, "Hey, it's a pretty good day—look at the sun shining through the trees!" He stretches his wings and decides to fly in the general direction of the wonderful smell. The smell gets better and better, and then he sees the female and immediately falls in love with her. They mate with each other, little eggs appear, and so on. What we feel in our stomach when we're in love is nothing but a chemical process. You can picture love as a chemical process, or as a beautiful poem.

Strangely enough, when we think about people in love, we tend to think about poetry, but with animals we think about chemistry. But during mating season you can see that animals lose their minds just like people in love. In the past, the spiritual life of animals was denied; people even thought that animals didn't feel pain. Yes, it's a bit of a stretch to think that every tapeworm has the same spiritual life as a person. But animals do know sensation, just like human beings. When you look at a clump of bacteria under the microscope, and you add some sugar with a dropper, the bacteria will come toward it, because they like sugar. When you add vinegar, they'll move away. That's a sign of sensation, even if it's very small. And although bacteria don't have nervous systems, I still believe that we should not put vinegar on them unless absolutely necessary.

Do animals have souls?

? *The Philosopher:*

Absolutely. The soul is the name for all kinds of things that are expressed through the body but seem to be something else. For example, you can push a body, but you can't push a thought. A punch on the shoulder hurts your shoulder, but the word "jerk" hurts your soul. Animals experience the same thing. A dog can break his leg, which is a typically physical thing, or he can sit and whine when he's at home alone. I think that he is sad, and that it's something more than a toothache. With people it's even clearer. You can kick a ball using your foot, or you can make a plan to play soccer tomorrow using your mind. Your head takes up space, but how much space does a thought take up? Or a plan? How much does a question weigh? Where is sadness located?

According to Aristotle, having a soul is the same as being alive. A dead body takes up just as much space as a living body. But it doesn't move, doesn't feel pain, doesn't think, doesn't make plans, and doesn't object to things. The soul is the difference between a living and dead body. The word "psyche" means "soul" in Greek. "Psychès" means "having a soul," and it also means being alive. "Apsychès" means dead.

⊂ The Pastor:

If animals didn't have souls, they would be poor creatures. The concept of the soul is the recognition of dignity. There were times when people thought that women didn't have souls. There were times when some people thought that non-Caucasian people didn't have souls.

✡ The Rebbetzin:

Animals have souls, but at a different level than humans. Plants and minerals also have souls. The soul of a rock is the power that ensures that the rock can exist.

☾ The Imam:

Not everyone knows what a soul is. For a Muslim, the soul is something like an invisible gas or fluid that is everywhere and nowhere in each person. Psychologists, also known as "shrinks," think that we reveal our

souls through our actions, or our dreams. Muslims practice rituals such as prayer and fasting to focus their souls on God, because they think that this is where the soul comes from. Animals also have a soul, because it is an essential aspect of life. Animals are also God's creatures. An animal without a soul would be pitiful.

Notes

Chapter 3
Emotions

You're angry, scared, or happy for a reason.

You have emotions in order to survive.

Let's talk about sadness, happiness, and love.

What are emotions?

🦁 *The Psychologist:*

Emotions make you react to important situations. When you're afraid, you run. Anger makes you aggressive, so you can chase others away if necessary. Positive emotions such as happiness make you see beyond the end of your nose. You become more creative and open to others; you want to make contact, and that's how you gain new experiences.

🎭 *The Cabaret Performer:*

When I read the poet Szymborska, my eyes often fill with tears. Other times I may I start to laugh uncontrollably. Why is that exactly? Sometimes I perform onstage night after night, and I always know exactly when the laughs will come. Everybody always laughs at the same time, even though the audience hasn't agreed when to laugh. Once, I went to the funeral of the father of a childhood friend. My

friend's father had certainly been a very nice man, but I hadn't seen him in years. At his funeral, I was standing in the back of the room, and all of a sudden I started crying so hard I couldn't stop. Later, I realized that I had been crying for the end of my youth, the time when I was always in love, when I got my moped, when I could still smell the forest where I grew up. You can't control your emotions; sometimes you don't know whether to laugh or cry. You don't always know why something is funny or pleasant.

Why am I sometimes sad?

🐗 *The Psychologist:*

You feel sadness when you lose something that was fun or nice, or something you were attached to. Or when you have to pass up on something pleasant. The emotion you feel then is painful, a feeling of helplessness and being left alone.

When you feel something painful, you usually call for help by crying. A baby mouse cries when it falls from the nest so its mom can pick it up and return it to the nest. But people also cry when we're sad and there's really nothing anyone can do to help us. When a person dies, that person isn't going to come back, no matter how hard we cry. In this case, crying is actually useless, but we still do it. Crying in people, by the way, is not only meant as a call for help: tears can also inhibit aggression in other people, because they make you more endearing. When you're crying, you're showing your vulnerability, and in a way you're actually asking for help. Just like that baby mouse who fell from the nest. Or even when you hear beautiful music that makes you cry. You're obviously not asking for help, but you are letting your guard down, which can make people feel more sympathetic toward you.

The Psychologist:

Anger appears in every animal or person who experiences other people bothering him. Anger calls you to self-defense or resistance. When you're angry, your blood pressure goes up, your heartbeat increases, and your muscles tense, so you can jump to action. You stand up straight, clench your fists, and open your eyes wide. Sometimes you'll scream or stamp your feet to make your point. You show that you should be taken seriously and that you're in charge.

The Brain Expert:

American researchers asked people to write down once a week whether they were happy. That's how they found out that happiness is very consistent in most people. Whether a person wins the lottery and becomes very rich, or has a terrible accident and becomes disabled, after a year that person is often just as happy or unhappy as before. So in the long run, events like getting rich or becoming disabled don't change your happiness.

This news only makes unhappy people even unhappier, though. The fact is, this research suggests that happiness is mostly inside of us. But where? When you study the people who say they're happy, one common factor is that they have many good friends. So, obviously,

friends are very important to consistent happiness. But in order to be able to bond with people and build strong friendships, certain centers in your brain must be sensitive to the hormones oxytocin (in women) and vasopressin (in men). This sensitivity starts in infancy. People who nurture and cuddle their children increase their children's sensitivity.

The Psychologist:

The experience of happiness involves completely losing yourself in what makes you happy, as well as losing your self-consciousness. You reach a state where you want to stay. Your thoughts don't revolve around you, and everything seems to flow. That's why people often don't realize that they're happy, because recognizing your own happiness can actually be a distraction from your absorption in your happiness.

How can I be happy?

? *The Philosopher:*

Happiness is a delicate game. If you plan to be happy, it usually doesn't work. Most philosophers advise achieving happiness in a roundabout manner. According to Aristotle, everyone on earth has a purpose hidden somewhere inside each of us. That purpose is to be happy. Aristotle said that if you use all your talents in the right way, you'll be happy.

The philosopher Immanuel Kant believed that you have to decide yourself which duty you want to take on, explain clearly what you intend, and keep your word. According to Kant, that's the highest freedom: don't do what somebody else says, but do what you say. Do your duty as a person. The British philosopher Jeremy Bentham had

completely different advice. According to him it doesn't matter if you use your talents (like Aristotle) or do your duty (like Kant), but instead you should always ask yourself, "What are the consequences of what I do? What will make the most people happy?" If you're not sure whether you should do something, just do the math: how many people will it make happy? The more happy people, the better your good deed.

So what's your best chance for happiness, in my opinion? Start your journey with Kant; continue traveling the road with Aristotle; and look toward the future with Bentham. My mother always said, "You should do one thing, but not fail the other." She was very happy.

✿ *The Buddhist:*

You can be happy by doing what you do really well. And doing it with attention—even the things that aren't a lot of fun. Moving around also helps to improve your thinking. Actually, the ideal recipe for happiness is meditating twice a day and exercising three times a week. That makes you very Buddha.

♀ *The Biologist:*

The foundation of happiness is desire. As a young man, I used to dream about Hawaii, where hula girls danced on the beach by the light of a

silvery moon. That image made me very happy. Now I know that you really shouldn't go to Hawaii for happiness; there are lots of tourists. The key word for happiness is harmony: harmony in body and spirit, harmony between you and your surroundings, harmony between your species and other species. Mind and body should be in balance; your mind is not more important than your body, nor the other way around. But there's no such thing as always being happy. There's no day without night, no summer without winter, and other such clichés you may find on plaques and posters.

 The Psychologist:

You become happy when you cross your own boundaries. You're happy when you achieve what you really want to achieve. The trouble is, when you put a rooster with a chicken, he wants to mate with her—but, unfortunately, after three times, he doesn't really like it as much anymore. And when another chicken walks by, he wants to mate with her. And after three times that isn't as interesting either. That's why we keep looking for new challenges in life and want to discover new things, and that makes us happy.

☻ *The Cabaret Performer:*

If only I knew, I would be happy every day. Very often you only know afterwards that you were happy. When I think back and remember summers at the seashore, they're wonderful memories. I was so happy then: playing on the beach and digging holes in the sand, covering them up at night, then digging them again the next day. Just like life itself.

? *The Philosopher:*

Plato said the following: man used to be a strong being with four arms and four legs. The god Zeus did not like that, because he thought that these strong men would be able to defeat the gods. So he cut all men in two, and we became creatures with two arms and two legs. The two halves, those incomplete men, kept longing for each other. They wrapped their arms and legs around each other to come together again.

All those incomplete men died from desire. Zeus felt sorry for them and made sure that the genitals were on the front of men, so one half would fit into the other and they would be able to be together again.

This is a story from Greek mythology, but being in love does feel like that. It feels a bit like coming home to the person who had always been part of you. As if together you were one.

 The Biologist:

Being in love is chemical pandemonium, a chain reaction of chemical substances which causes temporary madness. When you're really in love, sometimes you can't eat, and you can only think about your beloved. That infatuation has a biological function. Most animals avoid physical contact most of the time. People in the subway do their best to keep their distance from each other. But this presents a problem during mating season, because animals have to get together in order to procreate. It's an enormously strong power that keeps animals apart, and it requires an enormous power to bring them together again. During mating season, animals don't think about safety; they just go for it. In humans, we call this infatuation, or being in love. You experience being in love as a strange feeling in your stomach. It's not terribly pleasant, and it's occasionally disruptive. And it makes you write poetry.

The Brain Expert:

When you're in love, your brain starts to produce dopamine. Dopamine is a neurotransmitter that plays a huge role in feelings of enjoyment, happiness, and well-being. When you are falling in love with someone, you will only see that person's positive qualities. You will think that the person only says and does the most wonderful things, is very smart and funny, and—of course—very beautiful. Dopamine is like a drug, and it's addictive. So you need more and more to get that same pleasant feeling. At some point, when you have known the person for a while, the dopamine starts to wear off. The fact that people do stay together for a longer time is because during this phase of infatuation, other substances are also being produced in your brain: oxytocin (in women) and vasopressin (in men). These are known as "bonding hormones," and they help you attach to each other and have a longer relationship.

By the way, oxytocin is also released in the brain of a mother and her child when the mother breastfeeds or even cuddles her baby. It's also released when you become friends with someone. It causes defenses to drop, and allows you to let others get close. This is how a bond of trust and strong friendship is built.

The Psychologist:

Infatuation is the desire to always be close to a person, to look at the person and touch him or her, and to think that person is just beautiful. It also means being tortured by the fear that the person will reject or leave you, but feeling wonderful when you are together and the doubt is gone for a short while. Being in love is a kind of madness that seldom lasts very long. Novelty plays an important part in it. Infatuation wears off after a while. And thank goodness it does, because we can't live with that feeling indefinitely. When the infatuation is gone, the feeling may change into deep fondness or love for one another.

Notes

Chapter 4
Time

We always want to be on time. But what *is* time? If you think about it too hard, it might drive you crazy. Let's have the experts shed some light on the subject.

? *The Philosopher:*

The Roman philosopher Augustine said, "What, then, is time? If no one ask of me, I know; if I wish to explain to him who asks, I know not." In other words, it's hard to think about, and even harder to explain. For example, we know the Civil War happened after the Revolutionary War. But you could also say that people are always fighting wars. So things change "over time," but they also stay the same. This made Augustine dizzy: everything happens over time, but what makes up time itself?

People have been looking for time for at least 1,500 years. The philosopher Immanuel Kant said, "Time is not to be regarded as an object, but as the mode of representation of myself as an object." Time isn't a "thing," but is a way we perceive things. Time is a division we make ourselves.

We can make time visible when we put a clock on the wall, and we agree that an hour is sixty minutes and a minute is sixty seconds. Time can go really slowly—for example, when you're at the dentist. But time can also fly when you're having fun.

The Biologist:

Time is a way to make sure that things don't happen simultaneously. Imagine if there were no time; there would be Vikings *and* dinosaurs running around. It would be a mess. Time is a way to pretend that you're handling things one after the other.

The Brain Expert:

Time is also our internal clock. The biological master clock, a small group of nerve cells that arrange our daily and nightly rhythms, is in the hypothalamus. The master clock is one of the most fundamental principles in living organisms. It originated very early in our evolution, and it is very robust. When you remove cells from the brain, they will keep ticking for a few days. Even the most primitive single-cell organisms have clocks. Our clock is calibrated by the sun every day. People have an internal master clock of around twenty-four-and-a-half hours.

How about the
time difference
when you're flying?

The Brain Expert:

When you take a plane to another time zone, you feel out of sorts for a while afterwards. The same thing happens when you change the clock for daylight savings time. This is because the clock on the wall is no longer in sync with the clock in your head. For each hour that you move the clock, you need a day to adjust. So when you fly to Europe, where it is five to eight hours later, you need about a week to adjust your inner clock. When we fly through several time zones, our biological clock gets upset.

Can you travel through time?

The Astronomer:

When you look at the stars, you are actually looking back in time. That's because it takes time for light from other stars to reach us. The farther away galaxies are from us, the longer their light takes to reach our eyes. So the light we see from faraway galaxies is very old. We are in fact looking back in time and seeing the universe when it was still very young. A light year is often used to indicate the distance to stars and galaxies in the universe. It is not a unit of time, but the distance light travels in one year, and that's about 5,878,000,000,000 miles.

The Biologist:

In a way you can travel through time when you visit a place where time seems to have stopped. I live in a smaller town called Weesp because it reminds me of the city where I grew up, Amsterdam. Unfortunately, there is not much left of the Amsterdam of my childhood. Time passes

slower in Weesp. I pretend it's still the nineteenth century. I have turned it into a dusty old library, with heavy furniture and pharmacist bottles with embryos in formaldehyde. In the nineteenth century, the century I love so much, people still believed in progress. They believed in the future, and in all the emerging technologies that were supposed to make life better. They stood with one leg firmly in the past, and one leg firmly in the future.

? The Philosopher:

Yes, you can travel into the future by waiting.

The Brain Expert:

The journey there appears to take longer because your brain has to find the way. During the trip, it stores many details about the route.

On the way back, you use automatic pilot. The more new things you experience and turn into memory, the longer time seems to last.

Why does life go slower when you're young (or faster when you're older)?

The Brain Expert:

Life seems to go faster all the time, because we have fewer and fewer new experiences. When you're young, everything is new. You're at the carnival for the first time and on a mountain for the first time. When things are new, you look at them very carefully and you remember them well. Adults do many things they have already done many times before: going to work, or watching television, or going on vacation to the same place again and again. That gets kind of boring for the brain. It doesn't really register these things in great detail. Thank goodness you can do something about that dullness

(and about your perception of time). Just go somewhere else on vacation, or stay in different hotels on your vacation. That will automatically make your vacation seem longer. Getting a new job or making new friends can also extend your time perception in your life.

Notes

Chapter 5
Who am I?

Until the age of two, a child thinks he's part of his parents.

Then the questions start coming: why am I who I am?

What makes me, me?

🛞 *The Buddhist:*

The events in your life and your memories make you who you are. But it's also your parents, grandparents, children, and your appearance. And your preferences change continuously: things you liked two years ago you may not like anymore. It doesn't matter; you move on to liking something else. That's how you grow. So what or who are you? Is there anything that will always be or stay the same? Clearly not. In Buddhism, we don't know a soul as a constant value. There's only change. Continuous change from one to the other.

🔍 *The Biologist:*

You can only know who you are by comparing yourself to others. There are people with curly hair, people with straight hair, and males and females. That's how you can categorize, like a clerk in a hardware store. There are screws with round tops and square tops, flat heads and

Phillips heads. Biology is about similarities and differences. At the zoo, you'll see that some animals have things in common. That's why lions, tigers, panthers, and cheetahs often live together at the zoo. Then once they're in that collection, you can see their differences. Your identity is in what you have in common, but even more so in what distinguishes you. The fact that you're a human is a given, and whether you're a boy or a girl. But how are you different from other boys and girls?

It's important to know who you are. The substances in your body differ from the substances in somebody else's body. A good tracker dog can smell this, and can find you immediately.

The Brain Expert:

Deep within us there's the notion that those two arms and legs, that body, that voice, and those thoughts belong together. Together, they're one identity. Besides that you have your memories that tell you what you've done, who your friends are, what you're planning to do, what you're looking forward to, and what you had for dinner yesterday. Your memories enrich your sense of "me." Your name gets meaning mostly because others call you by that name. People call you, they say something to you, and that's how you're reaffirmed in who you are.

☪ *The Imam:*

In Arabic, "fard" means individual. It's actually one person among all other people. For Muslims, there is a different relationship between the group and the individual. The family bond is very strong. But thinking about yourself and who you really are is something that belongs to all cultures. This is the reason for the Arabic word "shakhs," which means person. This concept indicates that you can have your own opinion. A person is responsible for what he or she does. You might say that Muslim kids who grow up in the US think more about themselves than in a Muslim country, and because they hear how others feel about them, they start thinking that about themselves. Islam says that we should research ourselves. Everyone reflects on himself, but don't forget that "I" is also determined by the "you." "I" cannot exist without "you." If we want to understand ourselves, we must understand each other.

? The Philosopher:

No. Even if somebody is physically the same as you, he will always be somewhere else, at another school, with another pet, reading other books. He witnesses other things and has other experiences. And that's why he will never be the same as you.

Even twins don't experience the same things. Your interests also help determine what you go into. What do you love? If you're always playing sports, you'll grow up to be a completely different person than someone who always has his nose in a book.

Q The Biologist:

Is there someone else exactly like you? No, that is fundamentally impossible.

Who thinks inside of me?

Q *The Biologist:*

Thinking happens inside your head, in your brain. As an experiment, you could chop off your arm and you would still be able to think. This means that the power to think is not located in your arm. You could chop off your other arm and your legs, and on and on.

If needed, you could replace your heart with an artificial heart. And then you think, maybe those old philosophers weren't so crazy after all. It's as if there were a little man inside your head, somewhere near your eyes. He wears a hat and holds a stick, and that's how he controls you, as if he were in the cockpit of a large jumbo jet. Of course, that's not true. All this thinking, all your senses, all your humanness, are spread over your entire nervous system. Some scientists used to think that certain characteristics were located together inside your brain, like a place for

math and a language center. That's all nonsense. The sad truth is that all our senses, thinking, and loving are all scrambled throughout the entire nervous system. You can't separate them out; they're everywhere and nowhere.

 The Brain Expert:

Who thinks inside your head? Nobody. Your head thinks! Still, we do have the feeling that there's somebody inside there, a "me" who decides what we think, say, and do. Probably, the truth is like this: your brain tells itself what it's doing. It does so afterwards, like a movie where they add a narrator to describe the scenes. The sun comes up, you wake up and get out of bed. You feel hungry and eat. That's the story your brain tells you.

The story doesn't get written until somebody asks you why you're doing something. When nobody asks you, you just do it without thinking about it. This is how Buddhists try to live. Through meditation they practice not-thinking, which results in a very happy feeling, as if you're very close to yourself. We can experience this without meditation, too: when you're working on something in a very concentrated manner, then you're not wondering what you're doing. That's called "flow."

☪ *The Imam:*

In the Koran, people are encouraged to think, remember, commemorate, ponder, and consider. "Remember Me," God says, "and I will remember you." But thinking is very abstract. When do we really think? Can we really think? Easy to say, but how can you invite people to think? "Say what you think" has become very fashionable. But you have to be able to think.

Where was I before I was born?

✡ *The Rebbetzin:*

In the same place where you'll go when you're dead. Your soul existed before you were born. You can also have multiple lives.

☪ *The Imam:*

Even before a person is visible as a little seed, he is a soul in the world of souls. He will always want to return there. Man starts out as a little blood clot which attaches itself to the womb. Then it becomes a clump

of flesh in which the skeleton forms. The muscle tissue grows over it and, according to the prophet Mohammed, after four months the soul is breathed into that little person inside the mother's belly. The Koran says that the Creator asks all souls the question, "Am I not your Lord?" Everybody shouts unanimously, "Yes!" You also said "yes"—otherwise you would not be here.

The Brain Expert:

Before you were born, you were in your mother's belly. You had already experienced many things by the time you were born, especially during the last few months in the womb. Babies' brains are very active, though you don't remember any of it later. Usually, you can't remember anything from before your third year, but a three-year-old can remember what happened a year ago. So you can imagine that a baby remembers what he experienced inside the womb. This can be seen when babies react to sounds they heard inside the womb—like the voices of mom and dad, or the vacuum cleaner.

The Buddhist:

We don't come from nothing. You were already inside your mother when she was born, and she was inside her mother, and she in her mother, and so on.

And then you end up at the beginning of the very first life. You could say that you were created then, just like everyone who is alive now. Christians say that we are descendants of Adam and Eve. That's actually the same thing.

The Pastor:

In life there's purpose and purposelessness, and they are poles apart. Sometimes you can feel the purpose—say, when you're touched by a sad movie or a tasty ice cream. Sometimes things happen that seem to be without purpose, like a child dying. Perhaps that's because we can't quite see the whole picture. When you think that something is useless, perhaps you have isolated that event too much from other events. Sometimes we isolate death from birth, and from life. There's no parent who wants to miss out on the life of his child. Death has no purpose, but life does. It's comforting to always see the connection between events, even if that's not always easy.

☪ *The Imam:*

Yes, absolutely. Man is on earth to worship Allah. Feeling that He exists, that you want to get to know Him—that's the purpose of life. But two questions precede this. Why God? Why Creation?

Why don't we just let nature, its meaning and processes, stand on their own? Why do we need to introduce a "higher being" who only makes reality more complicated: a burden for our head, heart, and soul? And why nature? Why the wealth and fullness of existence; why no emptiness—pure, clean, innocent emptiness? That would be the easier from God's point of view, right? Perhaps every Muslim answers these questions differently, but the bottom line is this: there is no emptiness, and I feel and believe that there is a God. And I act accordingly.

Why are we on Earth?

🕎 *The Buddhist:*

To make Earth a beautiful place for you and for all others. A place where you enjoy being, even though it's not always easy.

✝ *The Pastor:*

When a child asks this question, you can tell him why you are on Earth. For example, "To love you and feed you and teach you what talking is. To love Daddy and to do my work well." This way, you'll encourage him to think about his own purposes in life.

☪ *The Imam:*

Each person is here to become a complete person. Man's ideal is not self-denial, but self-confirmation. And he can achieve that ideal by becoming more and more of an individual, more and more unique. And the prophet also said, "Create God's qualities in yourself." So you become a person by becoming a unique individual. Islam believes that

the larger your distance from God, the smaller your individuality. He who comes closest to God is the most complete person. But people among themselves need each other to become themselves. The Muslim view on mankind is not optimistic or pessimistic, but it sees man as having room for improvement.

The Brain Expert:

We are on Earth to be happy and to make others happy. People are very social creatures; you can see that in the brain. It is very important to have friends. After a good personal conversation with a friend, things in your brain have actually changed. Genes are being connected, so more of the substance serotonin is being produced, and that makes you relaxed and happy.

We were given enormous empathy to enable us to understand what another person wants and feels. You will often feel intuitively, for example, how you can help the other person to feel at ease. You can also feel someone else's pain: for instance, when your daughter gets a shot. It's also remarkable how many different faces we can remember! We can recognize thousands of faces. More than that, when you see a face you'll often immediately remember where you know that person from, what your feelings for that person are, and what the

other person knows about you. (Some people are better at this than others.) For example, you might say during a conversation, "Oh, I already told you that." Maybe this doesn't seem like a big deal, but we register and maintain a tremendous amount of knowledge. The same goes for voices. You might not talk with somebody for forty years, but when you hear his voice, everything falls into place.

Notes

Chapter 6

Sleeping and Dreaming

Most dreams are deceptive, although your dreams do say something about you and your feelings.

The Sleep Expert:

Every person needs sleep, on average seven or eight hours a day. Kids need more sleep than adults. When you're sleeping, it seems as if you're turned "off," but that's not true at all. Our bodies may be resting, but our brains are active. Depending on the sleep stage, your brain is somewhat active to very active. At the beginning of the night, during deep sleep, growth hormones are secreted which help to repair overworked neurons. Later, during REM sleep (or Rapid Eye Movement), neurotransmitters known as cholines are activated, and the brain becomes a closed network. This means that instead of processing information from the outside world, the brain focuses solely on processing internal information. This prepares us for logical thinking during the day.

The Dream Expert:

To rest. When we sleep, our body is limp, but in our head we're processing things that have happened during the day. Fun things and less-fun things. And you can see them in your dreams. If you couldn't dream, your head would become so full it would really stress you out. It's very important to sleep well and to dream in order to stay fit and healthy. Some people are good sleepers and some people are bad sleepers. Good sleepers function better during the day and are better at concentrating, so they perform better in school. Bad sleepers are more agitated, get in fights more often, and are more likely to develop depression.

The Brain Expert:

Sleeping also helps us remember things. The expression "let me sleep on it" actually means something. During the night, your memory is updated and events are placed in your memory bank. Your brain moves events from your short-term memory to the long-term memory. This doesn't happen in one night; it may take a while before something is really etched in your long-term memory. These events are being replayed again and again in order to record them so you can remember them well.

What happens when I'm asleep?

■ *The Sleep Expert:*

Your sleep consists of several cycles. You actually sleep and dream several times during the night, in different stages. Each sleep cycle consists of three stages and lasts around an hour and a half to two hours, depending on the individual. During each cycle, at some point you hit an important stage: REM sleep, when you dream. During REM sleep, your eyes move back and forth really fast behind your closed eyelids, and your brain is almost as active as it is during the day. It looks as if your eyes are seeing something, and this may be true—probably, your dreams. By the way, during REM sleep your muscles enter a state of near-paralysis, so you won't run out of bed to attack the opponent you're dreaming about!

Why do I dream?

■ *The Sleep Expert:*

Dreams ensure that you're able to get up in the morning and be energized to start the day. In your dreams you process things that keep you occupied and things that you have experienced. Dreams are also connected to placing new memories in your memory bank. Children experience more new impressions than adults, and they need to place these new impressions in their memories—especially the impressions that make them feel emotions. It's actually like this: the happier, angrier, or more afraid you are when something happens, the bigger the chance that you'll dream about it. And the greater the chance that you'll remember it.

Indigenous people often take their dreams very seriously and teach children at a young age to listen to their dreams. Suppose, for example, a person has dreams about being chased by a tiger. Over time they may learn to turn around and look the tiger in the eyes. That's how you can literally learn to face your fear. Dreams are always about our feelings, and when you learn to look at and listen to your dreams, you get a lot of information about your true feelings. And you process them as well.

A dream can also provide insight. All of a sudden you may understand why a friend is behaving a certain way. You may also have the courage to react in a way you wouldn't dare to do in real life. You might say something, for example, or suddenly feel very strong. This might make you feel a lot better in the morning and give you even more self-confidence.

The psychologist Carl Jung said that a dream is a letter from your subconscious. You wouldn't leave that letter unread; you would pick it up and learn from it. Dreams can give you insights into your feelings, desires, and thoughts. They are the answers from the subconscious, from your intuition. Listen to your dreams and you will live in wisdom.

Why do I have nightmares?

The Dream Expert:

Around Christmas there's a peak in the number of nightmares. This makes sense, because it's a very exciting time for young children, and they need to release this tension. It sounds terrible, but bad dreams can be very positive. They tell you something about yourself. A nightmare is no fun to process on your own. That's why a parent should invite a child to talk about it. But not at night, when it has just happened; instead, just comfort and cuddle them for a while. Don't do it in the morning, either, when everybody is in a hurry to get to school. Choose a quiet moment. Just a little chat. A parent might ask what the monster did in the dream and try to find out what is bothering the child, because he is actually talking about himself.

The Sleep Expert:

I had nightmares as a child where I was being chased by monsters, aliens, and bloodhounds. When it got too scary, I would wake up startled. My mom told me to try not to run away, but to turn around and chase them off. The next night, I was being chased by criminals. I was running and they were in a fast car with machine guns. I was terrified, but then I remembered my mom's advice. I turned around and stared straight at them. And they ran off. One of them even lost his hat.

I felt great—I had chased off four criminals! The moral: don't be afraid of confrontation. Chase your pursuers or have ice cream with them. Maybe they'll be nice! If you decide how to react before you go to bed, you'll be more likely to do it in your dream.

Do kids have different dreams than adults?

The Sleep Expert:

Everybody dreams about five to seven times a night, even people who don't remember their dreams. In total, children can dream around two and a half hours per night, and adults a bit less—an hour and a half to two hours. Children experience their dreams in a more intense manner. And they have better memories. They have more nightmares. Being chased, losing parents, angry monsters—nothing is too strange for a child's mind.

When a child is in a dark room and is staring at a dark crack in the wall, he will surely see a monster. Children dream about many things, but mostly animals.

Up to the age of five, children dream mostly about fantasy figures, such as elves, dragons, and monsters. Fantasy and reality are almost the same thing for them. From the age of six, children start dreaming about things they have experienced during the day. Friends and school play a large part. But the fantasy world still appears. Fairy tales, good and evil: these are major themes for children between the ages of five and eight. Adults have very specific dreams about colleagues, work, love, and relationships.

Are dreams real?

♫ Only in my dreams...

The Sleep Expert:

A dream is never real. A dream is a hallucination. It's as if you're watching a movie, but a really bizarre movie. You may, for example, dream about something that has happened to you in real life, but it never happens the same way. The story is taken completely out of context and all of a sudden other people appear in it. And they may change again into other people.

Because dreams are often very weird, you may actually find creative inventions or solutions in them. Your brain makes connections you may not have come up with in your daily life. The sewing machine, for example, was invented in a dream, and Einstein, Gandhi, Wagner, and Paul McCartney have found their best ideas in their dreams.

Can dreams predict the future?

The Sleep Expert:

We have never found proof of this. Chances are, on any given night, somebody will dream something that will happen the next day. People just dream about things that occupy them. During our lifetimes, we have around 150,000 dreams. Each night there are well over a billion dreams in the United States. Every once in a while there's bound to be a dream that seems to predict something.

Do dreams always have a meaning?

The Dream Expert:

Dreams are full of symbols, signals, and feelings that want to tell you something. Many books have been written about dream symbols and what they mean. I don't really believe all that. Dreams originate from your own feelings and perceptions. What may be a good symbol for one person may not be a good symbol for somebody else. If you love dogs, you will dream about dogs often and feel good about that. If you have been bitten by a dog in the past, then a dog in your dream will mostly mean a threat. You are the only person who can explain your dream. Children often find help in drawing their dream; all of a sudden they find their own meaning.

☪ The Imam:

In the Koran, two people ask Yusuf about the meaning of dreams. One of them saw himself pressing wine in a dream, and the other saw himself with bread on his head that was being eaten by birds. Yusuf explained the meaning of their dreams. He said, "One of you will be free and press wine for his employer, and the other will be hanged and the birds will eat from his head." One night, Pharoah had a dream that made a big impression on him. Nobody could explain his dream. When the wine presser heard about these dreams, he thought of Yusuf. He told Pharoah about Yusuf, and Yusuf explained the Pharoah's dream.

There is a whole dream-interpreting tradition in the Muslim world. A famous teacher once said, "Dreams are different because people are different." When you interpret a dream, each detail is important. Take water, for example. Water is usually a symbol for purity: clear water symbolizes solutions to problems; sweet, clean water indicates sufficient income or livelihood; murky water indicates an unhappy life. When you're watering plants or trees in a dream, this may mean that you will help other people, fight for the oppressed, etc.

Water flowing over muddy ground may indicate that you need to overcome an obstacle in your life. If you're washing clothes in a dream, this may refer to being freed from bad habits. Trees and plants are often

very positive symbols. If you dream about having a large, shady tree in your garden—even if you don't have a garden in real life—this may indicate a prediction of health or the birth of a positive person. A large, shady tree that falls over may indicate a death. A tree without leaves or fruit may refer to a setback or loss of profits or advantage. If you dream of a road or a railroad, this may mean that an obstacle has been cleared and that you have the green light for something.

Notes

Chapter 7

God

A man with a beard on a cloud? A bright light?
A universal power? No one knows what "God" is
for sure. But we can have some great talks about it.

Does God exist?

❓ *The Philosopher:*

God is created the same way as ghosts and monsters: with your imagination. But ghosts and monsters originate from your fears, while God comes from your ideals. If you have an idea about what goodness and beauty are, and you want the whole world to look like that, then you make an image of it. This image may be God. That's wonderful, because then you can adapt your life to this image. A beautiful, powerful image of what's good may serve as a guideline or a compass. When you behave accordingly, it will become reality. And then it works, literally.

😈 *The Cabaret Performer:*

Every night before I go to sleep, I pray to my god Ulekule. It's very easy to reach him, because he is never busy, as he has only one worshipper. Ulekule is a pretty lazy god and he thinks that one worshipper is more than enough. The other day, he said, "If you have more than one

believer, they'll just quarrel about who can be pope when you're not there." Ulekule is a very easy god. Ulekule doesn't demand anything. You can talk with whomever you want, think about stuff with whomever you like, and have sex with whomever you want. Even your husband doesn't let you do that. Really, Ulekule is the easiest god around. You may think, "I want him too!" Well, that's impossible. Ulekule is already filled up. The other day, somebody asked me, "That Ulekule of yours, did he also create you?" And I said, "No. It's the other way around."

What does God look like?

⤶ *The Pastor:*

Children often picture someone sort of like Santa Claus, with a white beard and a white robe, sitting on a cloud and looking down. You can only see His upper body. This image is wrong, of course, and after the

age of nine you lose it, or you spiritualize it. Spiritualizing means that you understand that something is a metaphor. We use metaphors to give God a shape. He is not like us people. But He's also not a Bang before the Big Bang. Nobody knows what God looks like; nobody has ever seen Him. God is a mystery, the secret behind everything. Christians believe that this incomprehensible God lives in love. That's how you can feel Him for a little bit.

✡ *The Rebbetzin:*

G-d is not a man with a long beard on a cloud. G-d is a power who makes sure the world exists. Sometimes G-d does strange things. You may think, why does G-d make war happen? But that's the mystery of G-d's power. It is almighty and you can't understand it. And you shouldn't want to, because that would place you at the same level as Him. G-d can't be grasped.

☾ *The Imam:*

We don't know. Because we cannot imagine God, there are no images. The shortest text in the Koran is about this subject: "God is one. He is independent. He was not conceived and does not conceive. And nothing or nobody is equal to Him in any aspect." The Koran doesn't say anything specific about making images or portraits, but Jews,

Christians, and Muslims are all rather opposed to idols. It's all about the one God. If you do wish to imagine God, I think the best way to imagine Him is as a kind of light. That's what He is called in the Koran: the light of heaven and earth.

∝ *The Pastor:*

Yes, there is only one God, but there are different religions. That's because people live in different countries, speak different languages, wear different clothes, and eat different foods. And that's why they also have different stories about God, and somewhat different images. If you say, "God is a father," somebody with a loving father will have a completely different feeling about this than somebody with a mean father. So our images are very different, but we all mean the same God. "Allah" is Arabic for God. We are all God's children—even the people who do not believe in God. They're not stupid or loveless, they just use other words to understand life.

✡ *The Rebbetzin:*

There's only one G-d, and that's G-d. If there were more than one, who would have created the others? And if the other gods were created, then they're not gods.

☪ **The Imam:**

There's only one. I mean that we are all talking about the same one. The word "Allah" simply means God.

? *The Philosopher:*

It all depends on the way you look at it. If you assume that we actually make our own God, then perhaps there are just as many gods as there are people. On the other hand, would we not all consider the same things as good? Everybody wants peace, everybody wants well-being, and everybody wants us all to have a good life together. This is a way to achieve a powerful and communal image of God. And when you look at it like that, it is also very easy to make a bridge between the different religions. Islam, Christianity, Judaism—they all want the same things.

⊰ *The Pastor:*

The world was created by the Big Bang, and mankind and animals have appeared on earth through years of evolution. So when I say that God created the world, I don't mean that He made it! What I'm really saying is, "I am amazed by the world, I feel respect for the world, I am grateful for the world." That is the metaphor that a child after the age of nine should learn to understand. Religion is not competing with science. It's a different way of experiencing the world. The scientist is looking for structures of cause and effect; the believer sings and speaks about his experience of worship and delight.

✡ *The Rebbetzin:*

First G-d created heaven and earth, and then light. He separated the water from the earth, which is how seas and pieces of land were created.

In the seas, He placed fish, and He let birds fly above. Then the animals on the land had their turn: the cows, horses, lions, and elephants. And then G-d created man. He did all of this with phrases, such as, "Let there be light." Of course, He didn't really say it like that. G-d doesn't have a body or a mouth; He cannot speak. G-d had an idea about what the world should look like, and when G-d has an idea, He lets it come into existence. You can picture it as a light with many lace curtains in front of it. In this world, there are so many lace curtains that you can no longer see the light.

By the way, you don't have to explain all this to a child of four or six or eight years of age. You can just tell him, "G-d did that." You should only answer the question a child asks and not give him any additional information he didn't ask for. What we as adults find difficult or what we have questions about, children in their innocence often simply accept. Don't give a child the explanation that you need, but what he asks for.

☾ *The Imam:*

Our creation narrative is almost identical to the story of the Christians and the Jews. Adam was alone. The fact that he was alone, and therefore one person, already holds a divine lesson in equality: we all originate

from the same ancestor. Still, it was better for him to have a spouse, an equal. That's why Allah created a woman from the same matter. In the Koran, we do not find Adam's rib. There is no cloning, but creating anew. Adam called her Hawa (Eve). Together they are the "parents" of humanity. Allah placed Adam and Eve in paradise, in the "garden," the Koran says. "O Adam!" it is said, "Dwell you and your wife in the Paradise and eat both of you freely with pleasure and delight of things therein." The only thing they were not allowed to eat was the fruit from a certain tree. But when something is forbidden, it automatically becomes extra appealing. So they both ate from the tree. In the Koran, Eve did not seduce Adam into eating from the tree; they ate together. And while they were eating from the tree, they became aware of their nudity for the first time, and they covered themselves with leaves. They realized they had made a mistake and begged for forgiveness: "Our Lord! We have wronged ourselves. If You forgive us not, and bestow not upon us Your Mercy, we shall certainly be of the losers."

God forgave them, but expelled them from paradise to earth, and said, "Get down, one of you an enemy to the other. On earth will be a dwelling place for you and an enjoyment, for a time. Therein you shall live, and therein you shall die, and from it you shall be brought out."

And that's how the history of man on earth started.

? *The Philosopher:*

Aristotle says, "Bickering is never about the goals, but always about the means."

☾ *The Imam:*

In the beginning, almost all wars have something to do with land, power, property, and resources such as oil. Religion is added to motivate people. The more emotion they feel, the more engaged they will be, so other people can maintain, win, or lose power.

Why do Muslims pray on rugs?

☽✦ *The Imam:*

It has to do with purity. When you're praying, you have to be clean. That's also the reason for ritual washing before prayer. You wash your hands, your underarms, your face, the top of your head, and your feet. Then you're ready to pray. The same purity also applies to the place where you pray. That's why you have to take off your shoes before you enter a mosque or the house of a Muslim. When you are praying outside or at work, for instance, you sit on your rug. Many of these rugs have a compass built into them. Muslims pray with their face toward Mecca, the Holy City. With that compass you always know the correct direction, no matter where you are. If you were to look down on earth from space, you would see Muslims at prayer appearing like iron particles pointing to a magnet. This creates a feeling of unity.

Why do Muslim girls wear headscarves?

☾⋆ *The Imam:*

Men and women are expected to dress "appropriately." These are codes that have to do with morality and chastity. This way, a woman shows that she's not interested in enormous freedom, and she's not available. And it works. Lots of boys won't approach a girl with a headscarf and say, "Want to go to a movie?"

On the other hand, such a concealment can also be extra attractive, especially when women put makeup on their eyes. And it's somewhat ambiguous. Men don't have to wear veils like women, as if men were automatically pure. But of course this isn't true. The truth is actually that women need to cover themselves because otherwise they would drive men crazy. But can't men control their hormones? Are all women objects of desire? And why are women burdened with morality and chastity when men can't control themselves? This also puts men in a

bad light. Men don't fall in love just like that with all women without veils. The problem with these rules is that they apply to the society of 1,400 years ago. They no longer apply to these times and this Western world. You can see in large Muslim cities such as Ankara, Cairo, and Casablanca that these rules are no longer applied very strictly. Men and women work together, and everybody is content. Women are just as educated as men. But when they are immigrants to non-Muslim countries, Muslims tend to abide more to the original rules. The country is new to them and, in their opinion, manners are sometimes too liberal. That's why they look for safety and security. And they find that in their own old traditions. This will slowly disappear.

Why do Jewish men often wear yarmulkes?

☆ *The Rebbetzin:*

The Bible says that a man should not shave his beard. The yarmulke, and the corkscrew curls Jewish men sometimes wear, are a traditional

costume. The way you dress demonstrates how you identify—both in connection to others, but also to yourself. The yarmulke is a sign that G-d is above us, beyond our understanding, and we cannot grasp G-d. There are also dress codes for women. Women shouldn't wear clothes that men wear, and their clothes need to cover their bodies. I would never wear short sleeves during the summer, because I want to emphasize the spiritual, not the physical. I don't want to distinguish between a beautiful or an ugly body. It's about the soul—what it does and means, and not what it looks like.

Notes

Chapter 8

Death

Everything dies.

Or does it? Let's talk about life after

death, heaven, and other comforting thoughts.

What happens when we die?

? *The Philosopher:*

We disappear. Life after death is the memory you leave behind with the people you spent time with during your life. If you make sure that it was nice to be with you, then your family and friends will remember nice things. And that's kind of like life after death.

♀ *The Biologist:*

When you've gone for a ride, you turn off the engine. The car still exists, but nothing functions. The big difference between a person and a car is that you can switch a car on again. When a person is switched off, he stays off. A person needs to always be switched on in order to stay alive. When you don't breathe for five minutes, or if your heart doesn't beat for five minutes, then you're dead.

The Brain Expert:

There are people who almost die, but at the last moment stay alive. That's called a near-death experience. Most people who talk about it say that it was a pleasant experience, a liberating moment filled with light and warmth. These people didn't really want to go back to living. Apparently, dying does something to your head that feels very pleasant. Nothing at all to be afraid of, obviously. But most of the time people are somewhat afraid of death, because they don't know where they're going. An English brain surgeon once described it this way: it's as if you're blowing out a candle. You're not going anywhere; a flame doesn't go anywhere after the candle is extinguished. It's just gone.

The Pastor:

When children ask me what happens after you die, I usually say, "That's a surprise from God!" We don't know. We can't know. But we hope that it will be good and beautiful. Jesus says the best way to prepare for Heaven is by living full of love, because love is the way to God. God doesn't ask anything else of us but that we try to do this. And this applies to all people, even murderers and thieves. Have confidence that death is all part of it, and that it's good.

✡ *The Rebbetzin:*

Every person has a body and soul. The dead body is put in a coffin in the ground and disintegrates, but the soul stays alive. The soul is something spiritual, which means that you can't perceive it with your five senses. You can't hear, see, smell, taste, or touch it. When somebody dies, you miss him—not his body, per se, but his presence. The jokes he used to make, the things he said. Everybody has a certain impact on the world and the people around him. When a teacher dies, everything he has taught his students will remain, and they will pass on this knowledge. That's how you can exist forever.

✺ *The Buddhist:*

I have no idea—I haven't died yet. Death is a big mystery and we simply don't know what happens because nobody has come back from death. We do know one thing: we will die. The only sure thing in life is that you will die. For Tibetan Buddhists, reincarnation is an entirely accepted fact. Reincarnation means being born again after your death because you still have things to finish up. After your death, you first go to a sphere where you face everything in your life you didn't finish processing. This may scare you, and you may run from it.

And you may run to the first womb you encounter if it's ready for impregnation. As you process more during your life and become less afraid, you won't run away so fast the next time, and you'll have the opportunity to chose a womb with better opportunities. And in a new life you'll have the chance to use these opportunities. Buddha himself did not worry at all about these issues. He believed that thinking too much about it could even limit you in trying to achieve enlightenment in your life here and now and live well.

Buddhism is about here and now, about this earthly life. You could say that paradise is here and not somewhere up there. There is no afterlife or a God who directs us; we have to do all of it ourselves, here and now. The art of life is that you learn to deal with what life brings you. Some things can be directed and changed, and in that case it's important to do so and find the courage and strength to do it. Other things can only be accepted, and in those cases it's important to have the patience to do so. That's why meditation is important: be quiet for a moment so you can better see what's going on and what would be wise to do.

♥ *The Cardiologist:*

My research of near-death experiences demonstrates that consciousness just "lives on" even when there is no visible brain activity. This leads me to the conclusion that even as the body perishes when somebody dies, the consciousness continues. This consciousness is the essence of life. I call it consciousness or essence, but you may also call it soul or spirit. Every culture or religion has a different name for it.

Where does the soul or consciousness go?

✡ *The Rebbetzin:*

G-d created the world. The first day, He made the boundaries between time and space. We think within that time and space, and are literally limited by them. The soul is not limited. The soul goes to a world

where time and space don't exist, the infinite. We cannot understand the infinite, although we try to find words for it. The soul is spiritual; it doesn't take up space and you can't ask where it is. The soul is everywhere and nowhere; it is beyond the limit of time and space. That is why it exists infinitely.

☪ *The Imam:*

Every Muslim believes in the afterlife. That's where both the body and soul go. This concept may be less clear for one person than for someone else. The Koran is filled with references to life after death. The afterlife is a paradise of pure joy. One person may desire earthly enjoyments such as rivers of milk and honey, and an abundance of fruits you can pick from the trees. Somebody else mostly wants to feel good and happy. For some people the highest goal is to only observe the beauty of God. In paradise, you will have eternal life. Actually, paradise is the same as heaven. We can't have a clear image of it. As a famous philosopher once said, "What would we do in that eternal Swiss sanatorium?" So in heaven we will be "other people" who do know how to enjoy eternity!

♥ *The Cardiologist:*

I assume that consciousness is everywhere in and around us. It's like the signals for the Internet and television. Those are electromagnetic

waves. When you turn on the TV, your TV will receive those waves and convert them into sounds and images. You can see a show. When you turn the TV off, the show doesn't stop; it just continues even though you aren't watching it. When you turn the TV on again, you can simply continue to watch it. It's the same with consciousness: it just continues, even if the body is dead.

Why do we die?

REST IN PEACE
JOHN WILSON

The Biologist:

You break down. At some point, everything breaks down; that's an important natural law, whether it's a fridge, car, or human being. When you drop a cup, it breaks into pieces. It won't just become whole again. Life is a one-way street; it starts at birth and ends with death. The funny thing about children is that they always want to be big. They have a

goal, something they want to do later on. And they have a devilish glint in their eyes, as if to warn their parents. But if you live long enough, eventually you are going to die.

☾ *The Imam:*

Life holds many secrets for us. How come we grow older? And why do we die? We don't remember the womb, and in the end we go into the earth, from which nobody has returned, either. Between these two mysterious places, our life takes place. For Islam, the origin of sickness, pain, old age, and finally death is the moment that Adam and Eve ate from the tree. Before then, they had eternal life, but they did not realize its value. Everything we experience here on earth is a test to see how we will do. After that, we may go back to our paradise. The Koran also sees it as something symbolic. When we went against God, we also died somewhat, spiritually speaking. To deserve heaven, we must come alive again, spiritually speaking.

✡ *The Rebbetzin:*

Apparently your task in this world is completed. Everybody is born with a number of tasks and potentials. It's up to you to either use those potentials or not. When you realize that G-d has created the world

and you as well, then you know that you will deprive the world if you don't develop your own talents. They are unique. Everybody has his own unique contribution. G-d has created us to do so. Sandwiches with peanut butter do not grow from trees. Corn grows, which is made into dough, which is kneaded and then baked in the oven. Only then do you have bread.

☸ *The Buddhist:*

Everything dies, even the sun and the stars. It is a law of nature.

♥ *The Cardiologist:*

All the people I have talked to who have had a near-death experience tell the same story: They were able to think very clearly, had memories

of their early childhood, and felt very content and happy, not at all afraid. Some of them left their bodies. They saw themselves lying with doctors around them. Many people saw a dark tunnel with light at the end. In that tunnel, some saw deceased people or some kind of creature of light. These experiences are universal; people with near-death experiences in each culture tell this story. Some say that it is caused by lack of oxygen at that moment. I believe that at such a moment consciousness works at full speed. More so, consciousness works better than ever when it's no longer stuck inside a body.

❀ *The Buddhist:*

One day, the Emperor of China asked a very wise Buddhist, "Where do we go when we die?" The wise man said, "I don't know." "Why not?" the

Emperor asked, disappointed. "You are a wise man. If you don't know, who does?" The wise man answered, "I haven't died yet, so I can't tell you."

We are born from a Power which we feel every day when we wake up in the morning, but we don't know where it comes from. We originate from this Power and return to it when we die. Hein Stufkens wrote a nice poem about this Power, and shows us we don't have to be afraid of it:

I was standing on the beach
Witnessing a misunderstanding,
When I heard two waves speak and say
Just before they hit the beach and went away.
One cried, "It is over and done,
We will break here and die!"
The other said decisively, "No way, you see;
You're not a wave, you are the sea."

The wave comes up (is born) and goes back to sea. After death we go back to the Big Power. Some call that God or heaven, others call it "Eternal life." Some Native Americans call it "The Eternal Hunting Grounds." We have always given a name to what comes after death.

Because of course we want to know where we will end up. But we can't really know.

For most Buddhists, it's not very important to know where we go after our life. For them, it's important to lead a good and useful life here on earth, and to respect other people, animals, and plants. Buddhists say, "If you live well, you can also die well," and you don't have to worry about what happens afterward. Death may be a very exciting adventure—who knows?

⌒ The Pastor:

Heaven doesn't exist somewhere in space. Heaven is an image that we have of afterlife. These images originate within time and space, but it's really all about what is outside time and space. Strictly speaking, the afterlife is noplace—because it is no "place"—and never—because it is not "ever." This is very philosophical, and a child is occupied with exploring his own world, which is purely physical. Adults who speak in two languages (they bury Grandma in the ground but say, "She's in heaven") should realize that for a child it's all one thing. The main question is, how can you offer a child a sense of safety and security in thinking about death? Most people use old-fashioned images to talk about heaven (clouds, castles) and say, "Grandma is up there, she

is a star or something." We know this isn't literally true—you could understand it poetically—but the child waves at the stars or releases a balloon at the grave.

One day, I was at a graveside with five children who had balloons to release for their grandmother, who had died. I said, "It's wonderful to release a balloon at this time, not because the balloon goes up to heaven, but the idea is that we have to let go of that balloon. When we let go of a balloon, it can choose its own way. That's how we learn to let go of Grandma. And we may trust that she is still in God, and that God loves her!"

The Biologist:

There is no heaven, but you can pretend there is. You can say to each other, "We'll meet again in heaven," and you can dream about that. Heaven could even be an important part of life, as long you realize at the end that it's a game.

♥ *The Cardiologist:*

I think that your consciousness continues living after your death. Life applies to everything here on earth that grows and flourishes. After death, there is existence. The consciousness continues. It is always in and around us.

☪ *The Imam:*

We don't know where we're going. It's a kind of intuition, an expectation. The Prophet said, "When one of you is dying, let him imagine the best of God and hope for mercy and forgiveness." In general, we say that only those people who can contribute to the inner calm of the person who is dying should be with him or her in the final moments. Don't speak ill of the dead. Within Islam we also only say good things about the deceased. We pray for his or her well-being in the afterlife. Assuming the grace of God is the entrance fee for paradise. That is why a Muslim who visits a dying person will try to direct his or her thoughts toward hope and peace with God and him- or herself, while reminding him or her of the Koran verse, "O you the one in complete rest and satisfaction! Come back to your Lord, well-pleased yourself and well-pleasing unto Him! Enter you, then, among My honored slaves, and enter you My Paradise!"

Will my bunny go to heaven?

🔍 *The Biologist:*

Secretly, this is asking if there is a heaven. A child thinks: a heaven where my bunny can't go can't be heaven. And I agree. I love cats, so I wouldn't like a heaven without cats.

The funny thing about these religious types is that they make up a heaven where there are no animals. That's very convenient, because then you don't have to deal with fleas, ticks, and tapeworms. First, people invent heaven, because they are afraid to die, and then they come up with the idea that animals aren't allowed, because they think that animals are a bit dirty. So they make up an excuse why animals shouldn't be allowed: animals have no souls like people, and only souls go to heaven.

Well, there's no such thing as a soul. The soul is an invention that was made up as a consolation for death. People don't want to die—and what do you do when you don't want something but it happens anyway? You deny it. The body dies; we can all see that— but hey, there's a soul, and no, you can't see it, and it will live on.

👁 *The Cabaret Performer:*

When our daughter, Anna, turned five, we gave her a rabbit. Fluffy brought her comfort and happiness in life. Fluffy went everywhere with her. Fluffy went to the supermarket, he went to the airport, and he went to our beach house. He had his own cage there.

One morning, I went to the cage and Fluffy was dead. I thought, I'm not going to sugarcoat this. So I went straight to the house and said, "Anna, I think something terrible has happened to Fluffy. Actually, I think he's dead."

We went to the cage and Anna started crying. By then, she was already fourteen. Big tears got all mixed up with mascara and left black smears on her cheeks. You couldn't have asked for a better transition from childhood to young adulthood.

I went to get my shovel from the shed and said that we would bury Fluffy in the yard. We play soccer in the yard all the time. And every time I score a goal, I make a cross in Fluffy's direction. I'm sure Fluffy is in heaven.

The Pastor:

Yes, your bunny will go to bunny heaven. And you can go there to visit Bunny.